Carry Your Umbrella

ISBN: 9798557160056

Dear Friend,

If someone gave you this book, even if it was a stranger, know that they must really LOVE you.

They love you enough to tell you about how much God Himself LOVES you!

I encourage you to put aside any notions of what you've HEARD about God, and read for yourself what HE says about Himself. And about you.

And what He did for you because He LOVES you more than you can understand.

What He did to make it possible for you to have a relationship with Him (the Creator of the universe) will boggle your mind.

And then when you are actually IN that unbelievable adventure of a relationship, your poor little mind will explode into a million stars when you sit down and contemplate how amazing He is.

(Don't worry, He can put your mind back together! LOL ☺)

Anyway, I hope you are as blessed in reading these pages as I was in putting them together.

Without you to read the words on the following pages, I have labored in vain!

So…

THANK YOU!

Blessings,

Beloved of the Lord

p.s. If you already profess to know Jesus Christ, I encourage you to read anyway.

The Bible says we are to test ourselves, to see if we are in the faith. This little refresher book might be of great assistance in that examination.

Before we begin...

For those new to all this, the words and numbers in parentheses tell you where in the Bible to find the verse I've quoted.

Example: (Romans 5:8)

Romans = which book in the Bible to look at

5 = which chapter of that book

8 = which verse in that chapter

If a book starts with a number, like this:

1 Corinthians 13:1

That means there are two books with the same name.

Confused? Fear not, and do not be dismayed! For I have typed out all of the verses for you!

Carry Your Umbrella

The Table of Contents

(The word "table" is in there to prepare
you for a feast! ☺)

Some Words From God

"So shall My word be that goes forth from my mouth; it shall not return to Me void, but it shall accomplish what I please, and it shall prosper in the thing for which I sent it."

~~~ **The One True God**

With great joy I present to you...

The Gospel! (The Good News!)

For God so loved the world that He gave His only begotten Son, that whoever believes in Him should not perish but have everlasting life.

For God did not send His Son into the world to condemn the world, but that the world through Him might be saved.

(John 3:16-17)

Taken from the beloved...

Bible! (Best-Selling Book Ever!)

For the word of God is living and powerful, and sharper than any two-edged sword, piercing even to the division of soul and marrow, and is a discerner of the thoughts and intents of the heart. **(Hebrews 4:12)**

All Scripture is given by inspiration of God, and is profitable for doctrine, for reproof, for correction, for instruction in righteousness, that the man of God may be complete, thoroughly equipped for every good work. **(2 Timothy 3:16-17)**

Heaven and earth will pass away, but My words will by no means pass away. **(Matthew 24:35)**

The grass withers, the flower fades, but the word of our God stands forever. **(Isaiah 40:8)**

It is written, Man shall not live by bread alone, but by every word that proceeds from the mouth of God. **(Matthew 4:4)** (Told you we'd feast! ☺)

Which was authored by...

God! (The Best Author Ever!)

God is Spirit, and those who worship Him must worship in spirit and truth.
(John 4:24)

But You O Lord, are a God full of compassion, and gracious, longsuffering and abundant in mercy and truth.
(Psalm 86:15)

For thus says the High and Lofty One who inhabits eternity, whose name is Holy: I dwell in the high and holy place, with him who has a contrite and humble spirit, to revive the heart of the humble, and to revive the heart of the contrite ones.
(Isaiah 57:15)

Let the heavens declare His righteousness, for God Himself is Judge.
(Psalm 50:6)

Before the mountains were brought forth, Or ever You had formed the earth and the world, even from everlasting to everlasting, You *are* God.
(Psalm 90:2)

And He...

Created Everything!

(Even lima beans for some strange reason. Thankfully, there is no command to eat them! ☺)

In the beginning God created the heavens and the earth.
(Genesis 1:1)

Have you not known? Have you not heard? The everlasting God, the Lord, the Creator of the ends of the earth, neither faints nor is weary. His understanding is unsearchable.
(Isaiah 40:28)

And His most cherished creation on earth is (believe it or not)...

Mankind! (That's us ☺)

(If He had gotten us through Amazon, He would have given us a 5-star review! ☺)

Then God said, "Let us make man in our image, according to Our likeness; let them have dominion over the fish of the sea, over the birds of the air, and over the cattle, over all the earth and over every creeping thing that creeps on the earth.

So God created man in His own image; in the image of God He created him; male and female He created them.
(Genesis 1:26-27)

And just wait until you see…

How He did it!

(Mind to the stars now! ☺)

And the LORD God formed man of the dust of the ground, and breathed into his nostrils the breath of life; and man became a living being.
(Genesis 2:7)

God gave him a beautiful home...

The LORD God planted a garden eastward in Eden, and there He put the man whom He had formed.
(Genesis 2:8)

And a lavish, tongue-tantalizing buffet for dining...

And out of the ground the LORD God made every tree grow that is pleasant to the sight and good for food.
(Genesis 2:9a)

He also gave him...

The First Job in History!

(Working for The Best Boss Ever!)

Then the LORD God took the man and put him in the garden of Eden to tend and keep it.
(Genesis 2:15)

However...

Regarding a particular tree...

The tree of life was also in the midst of the garden, and the tree of the knowledge of good and evil.
(Genesis 2:9b)

And the LORD commanded the man, saying,

"Of every tree of the garden you may freely eat, but of the tree of the knowledge of good and evil you shall not eat, for in the day you eat of it you shall surely die."
(Genesis 2:16-17)

Then God gave him his best gift yet...

A Woman! (We are a blessing! ☺)

And the Lord God said, "It is not good that man should be alone; I will make him a helper comparable to him."

Out of the ground the Lord God formed every beast of the field and every bird of the air, and brought them to Adam to see what he would call them.

And whatever Adam called each living creature, that was its name.

So Adam gave names to all cattle, to the birds of the air, and to every beast of the field. But for Adam there was not found a helper comparable to him.

And the Lord God caused a deep sleep to fall on Adam, and he slept; and He took one of his ribs, and closed up the flesh in its place.

Then the rib which the Lord God had taken from man He made into a woman, and He brought her to the man.

And Adam said:

"This is now bone of my bones
And flesh of my flesh;
She shall be called Woman,
Because she was taken out of Man."
(Genesis 2:18-23)

Bringing about...

The first marriage in history!

Therefore a man shall leave his father and
mother and be joined to his wife, and
they shall become one flesh.

And they were both naked, the man and
his wife, and were not ashamed.
(Genesis 2:24-25)

Then God blessed them, and God said to
them, "Be fruitful and multiply; fill the
earth and subdue it; "
(Genesis 1:28)

And all was well...

Then God saw everything that He had made, and indeed it was very good. **(Genesis 1:31a)**

Until...

The Temptation and Fall of Man
(aka The Screw-up Royale ☹)

Now the serpent was more cunning than any beast of the field which the LORD God had made. And he said to the woman, "Has God indeed said, "You shall not eat of every tree of the garden?"

And the woman said to the serpent, "We may eat the fruit of the trees of the garden; but of the fruit of the tree which is in the midst of the garden, God has said, you shall not eat it, nor shall you touch it, lest you die."

Then the serpent said to the woman, "You will surely not die. For God knows that in the day you eat of it your eyes will be opened, and you will be like God, knowing good and evil."

So when the woman saw that the tree was good for food, that it was pleasant to the eyes, and a tree desirable to make one wise, she took of it's fruit and ate.

She also gave to her husband with her, and he ate. Then the eyes of both of them were opened, and they knew that they were naked; and they sewed fig leaves together and made themselves coverings. **(Genesis 3:1-7)**

And that first sin brought about...

The Curse (The Bad News!)

So the LORD God said to the serpent: Because you have done this, you are cursed more than all cattle and more than every beast of the field; on your belly you shall go, and you shall eat dust all the days of your life.

And I will put enmity between you and the woman, between your seed and her seed; he shall bruise your head and you shall bruise his heel.

To the woman He said:

I will greatly multiply your sorrow and your conception; in pain you shall bring forth children; your desire shall be for your husband, and he shall rule over you.

Then to Adam He said, "Because you have heeded the voice of your wife, and, and have eaten from the tree of which I commanded you, saying, "'You shall not eat of it'":

"Cursed is the ground for your sake; in toil you shall eat of it all the days of your life. Both thorns and thistles it shall bring forth for you, and you shall eat the herb of the field.

In the sweat of your face you shall eat bread till you return to the ground, for out of it you were taken; for dust you are, and to dust you shall return."
(Genesis 3:14-19)

And although there was mercy...

Also, for Adam and his wife the LORD God made tunics of skin, and clothed them.
(Genesis 3:21)

There were also...

Severe Consequences (For all)

(Sucks to be us at this point of the story!)

Then the LORD God said, "Behold, the man has become like one of us, to know good and evil. And now, lest he put out his hand and take the tree of life and last forever"---

therefore the LORD God sent him out of the garden of Eden to till the ground from which he was taken. So He drove out the man; and He placed cherubim at the east of the garden of Eden, and a flaming sword which turned every way, to guard the way to the tree of life.
(Genesis 3:22-24)

As man multiplied, so did sin...

And this is what sin looks like...

For the wrath of God is revealed from heaven against all unrighteousness of men, who suppress the truth in unrighteousness, because what may be known of God is manifest in them, or God has shown it to them.

For since the creation of the world His invisible attributes are clearly seen, being understood by the things that are made, even His eternal power and Godhead, so that they are without excuse, because,

Although they knew God, they did not glorify Him as God, nor were thankful, but became futile in their thoughts, and their foolish hearts were darkened.

Professing to be wise, they became fools, and changed the glory of the incorruptible God into an image made like corruptible man---and birds and four-footed animals and creeping things.

Therefore God also gave them up to uncleanness, in the lusts of their hearts to dishonor their bodies among themselves, who exchanged the truth of God for the lie, and worshiped and served the creature rather than the Creator, who is blessed forever. Amen.

For this reason God gave them up to vile passions. For even their women exchanged the natural use for what is against nature.

Likewise also the men, also leaving the natural use of the woman, burned in their lust for one another, men with men committing what is shameful and receiving in themselves the penalty of their error which was due.

And even as they did not like to retain God in their knowledge, God gave them over to a debased mind, to do those things which are not fitting; being filled with all unrighteousness, sexual immorality, wickedness, covetousness, maliciousness;

full of envy, murder, strife, deceit, evil-mindedness; they are whisperers, backbiters, haters of God, violent, proud, boasters, inventors of evil things, disobedient to parents, undiscerning, untrustworthy, unloving, unforgiving, unmerciful;

who, knowing the righteous judgment of God, that those who practice such things are deserving of death, not only do the same but also approve of those who practice them.
(Romans 1:18-32)

Now the works of the flesh are evident, which are: adultery, fornication, uncleanness, lewdness, idolatry, sorcery, hatred, contentions, jealousies, outbursts of wrath, selfish ambitions, dissensions, heresies, envy, murders, drunkenness, revelries, and the like;

of which I tell you beforehand, just as I also told you in the past, that those who practice such things will not inherit the kingdom of God. **(Galatians 5:19-21)**

These six things the LORD hates, Yes seven are an abomination to Him: A proud look, a lying tongue, hands that shed innocent blood,

a heart that devises wicked plans, feet that are swift in running to evil, a false witness who speaks lies, and one who sows discord among brethren.
(Proverbs 6:16-19)

BUT...

The LORD is Merciful!

(It's about to <u>not</u> suck for us! ☺)

But God, who is rich in mercy, because of His great love with which He loved us, even when we were dead in trespasses, made us alive together with Christ (by grace you have been saved),
(Ephesians 2:4-5)

So...

He Sent Jesus, His One and Only Son

(aka our Knight in Shining Armor!)

Therefore the Lord Himself will give you a sign: Behold, the virgin shall conceive and bear a Son, and shall call His name Immanuel.
(Isaiah 7:14)

For unto us a Child is born, unto us a Son is given; and the government will be upon His shoulder. And His name shall be called Wonderful, Counselor, the mighty God, the everlasting Father, the Prince of Peace.
(Isaiah 9:6)

...He who has seen Me has seen the Father...
(John 14:9b)

You are from beneath; I am from above. You are of this world; I am not of this world.
(John 8:23)

He is the image of the invisible God, the firstborn over all creation. For by Him all things were created that are in heaven and that are on earth, visible and invisible, whether thrones or dominions or principalities or powers.

All things were created through Him and for Him. And He is before all things, and in Him all things consist.

And He is the head of the body, the church, who is the beginning, the firstborn from the dead, that in all things He may have the preeminence.
(Colossians 1:15-18)

Because Jesus was sinless, He is...

God's Sin Solution! (Salvation!)

But He was wounded for our transgressions, He was bruised for our iniquities; the chastisement for our peace was upon Him, and by His stripes we are healed.
(Isaiah 53:5)

For I delivered to you first of all that which I also received: that Christ died for our sins according to the Scriptures, and that He was buried, and that He rose again the third day according to the Scriptures, and that He was seen by Cephas, then by the twelve.

After that He was seen by over five hundred brethren at once, of whom the greater part remain to the present, but some have fallen asleep.
(1 Corinthians 15:3-6)

Therefore I said to you that you will die in your sins, for if you do not believe that I am He, you will die in your sins.
(John 8:24)

Jesus said to him, "I am the way, the truth, and the life. No one comes to the Father except through Me.
(John 14:6)

For there is one God and one Mediator between God and men, the Man Christ Jesus…
(1 Timothy 2:5)

And now…

He graciously reaches out to us…

(Take His hand when you see it! ☺)

Come now, and let us reason together, says the Lord, though your sins are like scarlet, they shall be white as snow; though they are red like crimson, they shall be like wool. **(Isaiah 1:18)**

To offer us…

Forgiveness and Redemption!

(Take it! Take it! ☺)

I, even I, am He who blots out your transgressions for My own sake.
(Isaiah 43:25)

Let the wicked forsake his way, and the unrighteous man His thoughts; let Him return to the Lord and He will have mercy on him; and to our God, for He will abundantly pardon.
(Isaiah 55:7)

But God demonstrates His own love toward us, in that while we were still sinners, Christ died for us.
(Romans: 5:8)

In Him we have redemption through His blood, the forgiveness of sins, according to the riches of His grace…
(Ephesians 1:7)

And…

Eternal Life with Him!

(Wait until you see what that looks like! ☺)

For the wages of sin is death, but the gift of God is eternal life in Christ Jesus our Lord.
(Romans 6:23)

Through…

Repentance!
(Turning <u>from</u> sin and <u>to</u> God!)

(A prayer with no turning won't help!)

Repent therefore and be converted, that your sins may be blotted out, so that times of refreshing may come from the presence of the Lord.
(Acts 3:19)

And…

He Sends Help for this Life!

(And there is no waiting list! You are always first in the que! ☺)

If you love Me, keep My commandments. And I will pray the Father, and He will give you another Helper, that He may abide with you forever---the Spirit of truth,

whom the world cannot receive, because it neither sees Him nor knows Him; but you know Him, for He dwells with you and will be in you.
(John 14:15-17)

However, when He, the Spirit of truth, has come, He will guide you into all truth; for He will not speak on His own authority, but whatever He hears He will speak; and He will tell you things to come.

He will glorify Me, for He will take of what is Mine and declare it to you. All things that the Father has are Mine. Therefore I said that He will take of Mine and declare it to you.
(John 16:13-14)

Then Peter said to them, "Repent, and let every one of you be baptized in the name of Jesus Christ for the remission of sins; and you shall receive the gift of the Holy Spirit.
(Acts 2:38)

So that...

We Have THIS Life ...

(You are crazier than me if you don't want THIS life! And I am Bipolar with Schizoaffective Disorder! ☺)

I have come that may have life, and that they may have it more abundantly.
(John 10:10b)

There is therefore now no condemnation to those who are in Christ Jesus, who do not walk according to the flesh, but according to the Spirit.
(Romans 8:1)

For as many as are led by the Spirit of God, these are sons of God. For you did not receive the spirit of bondage again to fear, but you received the Spirit of adoption by whom we cry out, "Abba, Father."
(Romans 8:14-15)

Peace I leave with you, My peace I give to you; not as the world gives do I give to you. Let not your heart be troubled, neither let it be afraid.
(John 14:27)

Until we get to...

THIS Fearsome Day!

Then I saw a great white throne and Him who sat on it, from whose face the earth and the heaven fled away. And there was found no place for them.

And I saw the dead, small and great, standing before God, and books were opened. And another book was opened, which is the Book of Life. And the dead were judged according to their works, by the things which were written in the books.

The sea gave up the dead who were in it, and Death and Hades delivered up the dead who were in them. And they were judged, each one according to his works.

Then Death and Hades were cast into the lake of fire. This is the second death.

And anyone not found written in the Book of Life was cast into the lake of fire. **(Revelation 20:11-15)**

And then we begin...

THIS Glorious Life...

(Not suicidal — tried that twice--BUT Oh! I can't wait to get to this part! ☺)

Now I saw a new heaven and a new earth, for the first heaven and the first earth had passed away. Also there was no more sea.

Then I, John, saw the holy city, New Jerusalem, coming down out of heaven from God, prepared as a bride adorned for her husband.

And I heard a loud voice from heaven saying, "Behold, the tabernacle of God is with men, and He will dwell with them, and they shall be His people. God Himself will be with them and be their God.

And God will wipe away every tear from their eyes; there shall be no more death, nor sorrow, nor crying. There shall be no more pain, for the former things have passed away."
(Revelation 21:1-4)

But I saw no temple in it, for the Lord God Almighty and the Lamb are its temple.

The city had no need of the sun or of the moon to shine in it, for the glory of God illuminated it. The Lamb is its light.

And the nations of those who are saved shall walk in its light, and the kings of the earth bring their glory and honor into it.

Its gates shall not be shut at all by day (there shall be no night there). And they shall bring the glory and the honor of the nations into it.

But there shall by no means enter it anything that defiles, or causes an abomination or a lie, but only those who are written in the Lamb's Book of Life. **(Revelation 21:22-27)**

And he showed me a pure river of water of life, clear as crystal, proceeding from the throne of God and of the Lamb.

In the middle of its street, and on either side of the river, was the tree of life,

which bore twelve fruits, each tree
yielding its fruit every month.

The leaves of the tree were for the healing
of nations. And there shall be no more
curse, but the throne of God and of the
Lamb shall be in it, and His servants shall
serve Him.

They shall see His face, and His name
shall be on their foreheads. There shall be
no light there.

They need no lamp nor light of the sun,
for the Lord God gives them light. And
they shall reign forever and ever.
(Revelation 22:1-5)

The Gospel (Good News)

For God so loved the world that He gave His only begotten Son, that whoever believes in Him should not perish but have everlasting life.

For God did not send His Son into the world to condemn the world, but that the world through Him might be saved.

(John 3:16-17)

When you repent...

Angels Rejoice in Heaven!

Likewise I say to you, there is joy in the presence of angels of God over one sinner who repents.
(Luke 15:10)

Because now you are...

Sealed with the Holy Spirit !

In Him you also trusted, after you heard the word of truth, the gospel of your salvation; in whom also, having believed, you were sealed with the Holy Spirit of promise, who is the guarantee of our inheritance until the redemption of the purchased possession, to the praise of God.
(Ephesians 1:13-14)

A New Creation!

Therefore, if anyone is in Christ, he is a new creation; old things have passed away; behold all things have become new.
(2 Corinthians: 5:17)

Adopted into God's Family !

For you did not receive the spirit of
bondage again to fear, but you received
the Spirit of adoption by whom we cry
out, "Abba, Father."
(Romans 8:15)

A Member of the Body of Christ!

Now you are the body of Christ, and
members individually.
(1 Corinthians 12:27)

A Part of the Bride of Christ, the Church!

Let us be glad and rejoice and give Him
glory, for the marriage of the Lamb has
come and his wife has made herself
ready.
(Revelation 19:7)

And He is the head of the body, the
church, who is the beginning, the
firstborn from the dead, that in all things
He may have the preeminence.
(Colossians 1:18)

Born Again into God's Kingdom!

Most assuredly, I say to you, unless one is born again, he cannot see the kingdom of God.

Jesus answered, "Most assuredly, I say to you, unless one is born of water and the Spirit, he cannot enter the kingdom of God.
(John 3:3,5)

In the Book of Life!

And anyone not found written in the Book of Life was cast into the lake of fire..
(Revelation 20:15)

In a Covenant with Him

Then He took the cup, and gave thanks, and gave it to them, saying, "Drink from it, all of you. For this is My blood of the new covenant, which is shed for many for the remission of sins."
(Matthew 26:27-28)

And also...

Set Free from Darkness

He has delivered us from the power of darkness and conveyed us into the kingdom of the Son of His love, in whom we have redemption through His blood, the forgiveness of sins.
(Colossians 1:13-14)

And if all that were not enough...

We are Joint Heirs with Christ!!

The Spirit Himself bears witness with our spirit that we are children of God, and if children, then heirs — heirs of God and joint heirs with Christ, if indeed we suffer with Him, that we may also be glorified together.
(Romans 8:16-17)

(If all that didn't excite you, follow these steps:

1. Go back and read it again.

2. Repeat step one until sufficiently awed! ☺)

So now, by the power of the Holy Spirit...

We Live a New Life!

(Now THIS is living life to the fullest!)

I say then: Walk in the Spirit, and you shall not fulfill the lust of the flesh. For the flesh lusts against the Spirit, and the Spirit against the flesh; and these are contrary to one another, so that you do not do the things that you wish.
(Galatians 5:16-17)

But the fruit of the Spirit is love, joy, peace, longsuffering,
kindness, goodness, faithfulness, gentleness, self-control. Against such there is no law.

And those who are Christ's have crucified the flesh with its passions and desires. If we live in the Spirit, let us also walk in the Spirit.   **(Galatians 5:22-25)**

Jesus said to him, "'You shall love the Lord your God with all your heart, with all your soul, and with all your mind.' This is the first and great commandment.

And the second is like it: 'You shall love your neighbor as yourself.'
(Matthew 22:37-39)

I, therefore, the prisoner of the Lord, beseech you to walk worthy of the calling with which you were called, with all lowliness and gentleness,

with longsuffering, bearing with one another in love, endeavoring to keep the unity of the Spirit in the bond of peace.
(Ephesians 4:1-3)

Therefore, put away lying, "Let each one of you speak peace with his neighbor, for we are members of one another.

"Be angry, and do not sin". Do not let the sun go down on your wrath, nor give place to the devil.

Let him who stole steal no longer, but rather let him labor, working with his hands what is good, that he may have something to give him who has need.

Let no corrupt word proceed out of your mouth, but what is good for necessary

edification, that it may impart grace to the hearers.
And do not grieve the Holy Spirit of God, by whom you were sealed for the day of redemption.

Let all bitterness, wrath, anger, clamor, and evil speaking be put away from you, with all malice. And be kind to one another, even as God in Christ forgave you.
(Ephesians 4:25-32)

Therefore be imitators of God as dear children. And walk in love as Christ also has loved us and given Himself for us, an offering and a sacrifice to God for a sweet-smelling aroma.

But fornication and all uncleanness or covetousness, let it not even be named among you, as is fitting for saints; neither filthiness, nor foolish talking, nor course jesting, which are not fitting, but rather giving of thanks.
(Ephesians 5:1-4)

You need to know...

About Your Powerful Enemy

(He HATES you with a passion beyond any human hate you've ever known!)

But I fear, lest somehow, as the serpent deceived Eve by his craftiness, so your minds may be corrupted from the simplicity that is in Christ.
(2 Corinthians 11:3)

You are of your father the devil, and the desires of your father you want to do. He was a murderer from the beginning, and does not stand in the truth, because there is no truth in him.

When he speaks a lie, he speaks from his own resources, for he is a liar and the father of it.
(John 8:44)

And then the lawless one will be revealed, whom the Lord will consume with the breath of His mouth and destroy with the brightness of His coming.

The coming of the lawless one is according to the working of Satan, with all power, signs, and lying wonders, and

with all unrighteous deception among those who perish, because they did not receive the love of truth, that they might be saved.
(2 Thessalonians 2:8-12)

Then he showed me Joshua the high priest standing before the Angel of the LORD, and Satan standing at his right hand to oppose him.

And the LORD said to Satan, "The LORD rebuke you, Satan! The LORD who has chosen Jerusalem rebuke you! Is this not a brand plucked from the fire?"
(Zechariah 3:1-2)

Be sober, be vigilant; because your adversary the devil walks about like a roaring lion, seeking whom he may devour.
(1 Peter 5:8)

For Satan himself transforms himself into an angel of light.
(2 Corinthians 11:14)

But Take Heart!

For this purpose the Son of God was manifested, that He might destroy the works of the devil.
(1 John 3:8b)

Because in the end...

(Which many believe will be soon! ☺)

The devil, who deceived them, was cast into the lake of fire and brimstone where the beast and the false prophet are. And they will be tormented day and night forever.
(Revelation 20:10)

In the meanwhile...

Wage Warfare!

Therefore submit to God. Resist the devil and he will flee from you.
(James 4:7)

Finally, my brethren, be strong in the Lord and in the power of His might. Put on the whole armor of God, that you may be able to stand against the wiles of the devil.

For we do not wrestle against flesh and blood, but against principalities, against powers, against rulers of the darkness of this age, against spiritual hosts of wickedness in the heavenly places.

Therefore take up the whole armor of God, that you may be able to withstand in the evil day, and having done all, to stand.

Stand therefore, having girded your waist with truth, having put on the breastplate of righteousness, and having shod your feet with the preparation of the gospel of peace;

above all, taking the shield of faith with which you will be able to quench all the fiery darts of the wicked one.

And take the helmet of salvation, and the sword of the Spirit, which is the word of God; praying always with all prayer and supplication for all the saints...
(Ephesians 6:10-18)

And finally....

Come to Me, all you who labor and are heavy laden, and I will give you rest.

Take My yoke upon you and learn from Me, for I am gentle and lowly in heart, and you will find rest for your souls.

For My yoke is easy and My burden is light."

~~~ **The Lord Jesus Christ**

Some Words

From

Beloved of the Lord

Dear Friend,

It has been a privilege and an honor to share God's love with you by sharing His precious word.

I will be showing you more Scripture verses, but now I will be adding a little commentary of what I've learned from my journey with Jesus.

If you saw your need for forgiveness through Christ in the first part of this book and chose to repent, then I a send you a heartfelt welcome to the family of God! ☺

God's love for you knows no bounds and nothing can separate you from that love! Sound too good to be true? Check it out!

For I am persuaded that neither death nor life, nor angels nor principalities nor powers, nor things present nor things to come, nor height nor depth, nor any other created thing, shall be able to separate us from the love of God which is in Christ Jesus our Lord.
(Romans 8:38-39)

If you have truly chosen to repent, you have been restored to a right relationship with your Creator. Like any other relationship, you grow more and more intimate as you spend time together getting to know one another.

God already knows everything about you. He knows every thing you've ever done and every thought you've ever had. But O the JOY you will find in the blessing of getting to know Him! ☺

I cannot stress enough the importance of knowing Him **personally**, as opposed to merely knowing **about** Him.

You can know the whole Bible by heart, go to church every time the door is open, give all your time and money to charity, and still miss the whole point of redemption and restoration.

But let him who glories glory in this, that he understands and knows Me, that I am the LORD, exercising lovingkindness, judgment, and righteousness in the earth. For in these I delight," says the LORD.
(Jeremiah 9:24)

And now the question arises, "How do I get to know Him personally?"

So glad you asked! ☺

Prayer is the answer! Prayer is simply talking to God. And — here is the REALLY exciting part! — God talking to you!

Can it get any better than that? Or any easier than that? Our Lord has made things so simple for us, yet we humans are always trying to complicate everything.

The Bible gives us LOTS of encouragement on how to pray and what to pray for, but I am only going to share a few.

God's children have the privilege of approaching His throne with boldness (not to be confused with arrogance ☺).

Let us therefore come boldly to the throne of grace, that we may obtain mercy and find grace to help in time of need.
(Hebrews 4:16)

We have confidence that He will hear us!

Now this is the confidence that we have in Him, that if we ask **anything according to His will**, *He hears us. And if we know that He hears us, whatever we ask, we know that we have the petitions that we have asked of Him.*
(1 John 5:14-15 emphasis mine)

We can pray about everything and anything! Thankful that God will answer in the way He sees best!

Be anxious for nothing, but in everything by prayer and supplication, with thanksgiving, let your requests be made known to God;
(Philippians 4:6)

We are to pray in good times and in bad.

Is anyone among you suffering? Let him pray. Is anyone cheerful? Let him sing psalms.
(James 5:13)

(Sing any song you like to the Lord! I make up my own all the time and He loves it! ☺)

This next one is one of my all-time favorite verses on prayer. (I have a big grin on my face as I type this one out. LOL ☺)

But you, when you pray, go into your room, and when you have shut your door, pray to your Father who is in the secret place; and your Father who sees in secret will reward you openly.
(Matthew 6:6)

Believing the Lord's words in this verse will strengthen your faith in ways that I cannot even explain!

There is nothing like the feeling of having a secret prayer going with the Lord and Him blowing your mind to the stars by answering it in a way that was plainly Him.

There is a time and a place for sharing your prayer requests with others who will pray for and with you. It is very important to do so.

But...

It is also very important to keep some to yourself. This way you can see God answer, and know that only He could have brought that about.

It is SO exciting when that happens!! And the more you pray, the more it happens!

Rejoice always, pray without ceasing, in everything give thanks; for this is the will of God in Christ Jesus for you.
(1 Thessalonians 5:16-18)

(Just to clarify, if you have a place to get away where it is quiet and private...hooray! But if not, secret prayers in your head are still rewarded openly!)

Are you worried that you don't know the right words to pray? Then I've got great news for you!

Just use the words you have. You don't have to be eloquent, or a Bible scholar, or a preacher; you just have to be you, and you have to be honest.

Once again, the Lord makes it so simple!

Still not feeling too confident? Fear not!
Instead of using your words, use His! ☺

I'll give you an example.

Let's say you want to pray for someone
who doesn't yet know Jesus personally.
(A most important prayer!)

Hmmm. We'll say your kid brother and
we'll name him, Matthew. Then we'll say
when you were kids you called him,
"Tubaloaf."

And to add to the story, we'll say that by
his own choice he is estranged from your
family and you are heartbroken.

We'll use this verse from Isaiah:

Let the wicked forsake his way,
And the unrighteous man his thoughts;
Let him return to the Lord,
And He will have mercy on him;
And to our God,
For He will abundantly pardon.
(Isaiah 55:7)

My prayer based on this verse would
look something like this:

Lord, I come to You today to ask You for mercy for my brother. We both know that he still walks in his own way.

According to Your word, he is still unrighteous. Please have mercy on him, Lord. Help him find his way to return to You.

Please send someone to tell him about how You are our God, the true God, and to tell him about how you abundantly pardon.

Please do it quickly, Lord. I miss and love my Tubaloaf so much.

I ask this in the name of Your Son, Jesus, and I thank You for hearing me. Amen.

******

And just like that I've prayed a Scripture! I really hope you have been encouraged to pray!

And here's another beautiful prayer passage I want to add in:

Who then is the one who condemns? No one.
Christ Jesus who died – more than that, who
was raised to life – is at the right hand of
God and is also interceding for us.
(Romans 8:34)

Yes, you read that right. If you belong to Him, Jesus Christ Himself is praying for you.

How can anything be more encouraging than that?? ☺

As you adventure through the Bible you will find many examples of prayer being answered in amazing ways. And that's because God is AMAZING! ☺

Check THIS out!

It shall come to pass
That before they call, I will answer;
And while they are still speaking I will hear.
(Isaiah 65:24)

Yes! God knows your prayer before you even ask it, and if it is according to His will, He is already answering it!

It should be noted that God will not always answer our prayers the way we think He will, or want Him to, or expect Him to.

And sometimes He just flat out says, "No."

That is where you need to just trust Him. He knows you WAY better than you know yourself, so trust that He knows what is best for you.

Also, we humans tend to get caught up in prayers for all kinds of selfish (sinful) things.

You ask and do not receive, because you ask amiss, that you may spend it on your pleasures.
(James 4:3)

We are taught to pray for everything, and this includes our material needs, but we are also taught this little gem regarding worrying about what we are going to eat, and drink, and wear:

For your heavenly Father knows that you need all these things.

But seek first the kingdom of God and His righteousness, and all these things shall be added to you.
(Matthew 6:32-33)

There is one thing that will stop the Lord God from answering your prayers. Sin.

But your iniquities have separated you from your God;
And your sins have hidden His face from you,
So that He will not hear.
(Isaiah 59:2)

Fear not! Although the Bible is plain that we will still sometimes struggle with sin, even though we are now in Christ, God has a remedy!

If we confess our sins, He is faithful and just to forgive us our sins and to cleanse us from all unrighteousness.

If we say that we have not sinned, we make Him a liar, and His word is not in us.
(1 John 1:9-10)

And guess what? Although receiving what we ask for is an answer to prayer, and in our circumstances He answers prayer, He also answers through His word, the Bible!

It should be obvious throughout this book that I believe with my whole heart that the Bible is the word of God.

It should also be obvious that this whole book is based on three Scriptures listed right at the beginning.

Don't turn back! I'll put them here again!

So shall My word be that goes forth from My mouth; It shall not return to Me void, But it shall accomplish what I please, And it shall prosper in the thing for which I sent it.
(Isaiah 55:11)

For the word of God is living and powerful, and sharper than any two-edged sword, piercing even to the division of soul and spirit, and of joints and marrow, and is a discerner of the thoughts and intents of the heart.
(Hebrews 4:12)

All Scripture is given by inspiration of God, and is profitable for doctrine, for reproof, for correction, for instruction in righteousness, that the man of God may be complete, thoroughly equipped for every good work.
(2 Timothy 3:16-17)

(The word "doctrine" means "teaching," or "teaching to make one wise." Thankful God sees fit to give us that! ☺)

I don't know how I can possibly explain that any clearer than it is, but I will say something regarding "instruction in righteousness."

That applies to your WHOLE life!! Now that you are in Christ, God wants you to live a life of righteousness. The Bible has the instructions for that! Yippee!!

But don't forget! You can't do it without the power of the Holy Spirit.

As you read His instructions, pray that you would be sensitive to His Spirit's leading so that you will be able to live the life He is calling you to!

Also, as you see the areas in which you fall short, confess that as sin and ask for forgiveness! Receive it and be cleansed like we just talked about!

If you attempt to live a godly life in your own strength, without relying on the Holy Spirit to lead and change you, you will fail.

Worse than that, you will not be able to keep up the façade, and will become a hypocrite.

A person preaching one thing and living a completely different way. Trust me — that sucks.

Been there and done that for a very long time. I praise and thank God for His mercy in delivering me from myself.

I have done horrible things while professing to be a believer in Christ. I have since repented and been truly reconciled to Him.

His forgiveness is total and complete as my repentance is real, but I have learned a valuable lesson.

Even though Jesus rejoices to truly have me back, many people have not forgiven me for some of the things I've done.

The unbelievers I understand, but the professing Christians I don't. I am not bringing this up to complain about them (on the contrary, I pray for them), but to share something very important with you.

The topic of forgiveness.

Mercy and forgiveness go hand-in-hand. It is because God is merciful that He made a way for us to be forgiven without compromising His righteous judgment upon our sin.

The Bible has a lot to say about forgiveness. How our loving, merciful, and gracious God forgives us, and how we are to lovingly, mercifully, and graciously forgive others.

Like our heavenly Father. And like our Savior. That's how.

One of Jesus' disciples asked Him how often he needed to forgive someone. Jesus replied with the following parable:

Therefore the kingdom of heaven is like a certain king who wanted to settle accounts with his servants.

And when he had begun to settle accounts, one was brought to him who owed him ten thousand talents.

But as he was not able to pay, his master commanded that he be sold, with his wife and children and all that he had, and that payment be made.

The servant therefore fell down before him, saying, 'Master, have patience with me, and I will pay you all.' Then the master of that servant was moved with compassion, released him, and forgave him the debt.

"But that servant went out and found one of his fellow servants who owed him a hundred denarii; and he laid hands on him and took him by the throat, saying, 'Pay me what you owe!'

So his fellow servant fell down at his feet and begged him, saying, 'Have patience with me, and I will pay you all.' And he would not, but went and threw him into prison till he should pay the debt.

So when his fellow servants saw what had been done, they were very grieved, and came and told their master all that had been done.

Then his master, after he had called him, said to him, 'You wicked servant! I forgave you all that debt because you begged me. Should you not also have had compassion on your fellow servant, just as I had pity on you?'

And his master was angry, and delivered him to the torturers until he should pay all that was due to him.

"So My heavenly Father also will do to you if each of you, from his heart, does not forgive his brother his trespasses."
(Matthew 18:23-35)

The king in that story represents the true King, the Lord. The first servant represents you. And me. And every person who has called upon the name of Jesus for forgiveness.

The ten thousand talents are like a gazillion dollars that the servant didn't have. And would never have. He owed a large debt that he could never repay.

Yet, he was forgiven.

Then he goes out and shakes down a fellow servant for five bucks that is owed to him.

Take a good look at his hard heart and his end result. Do not be that servant.

Hear again, and heed the warning of Jesus:

"So My heavenly Father also will do to you if each of you, from his heart, does not forgive his brother his trespasses."
(Matthew 18:35)

That warning is very similar to His words in these verses from the gospel of Mark:

"And whenever you stand praying, if you have anything against anyone, forgive him,

that your Father in heaven may also forgive
you your trespasses.

But if you do not forgive, neither will your
Father in heaven forgive your trespasses."
(Mark 11:25-26)

Someone very important in the Bible
penned this:

I have hidden Your word in my heart, that I
might not sin against You.
(Psalm 119:11)

I strongly encourage you to get the story
you just read deep into your heart.

Also, do not neglect to ask forgiveness
when you are the offender.

Therefore if you bring your gift to the altar,
and there remember that your brother has
something against you, leave your gift there
before the altar, and go your way. First be
reconciled to your brother, and then come
and offer your gift.
(Matthew 5:23-24)

They may or may not forgive you, but
right the wrongs that you can and leave

the rest in God's loving, gracious, and merciful hands.

One last thing on forgiveness, and please get this one deep in your heart, too.

Meditate on and contemplate our Lord's prayer for those who mercilessly mocked, beat, and whipped Him, before nailing Him to a cross.

And when they had come to the place called Calvary, there they crucified Him, and the criminals, one on the right hand and the other on the left.

Then Jesus said, "Father, forgive them, for they do not know what they do.
(Luke 23:33-34a)

Jesus is the heart of the gospel; and the heart of Jesus toward us is forgiveness.

Prayer and forgiveness. Forgiveness and prayer.

These two things, hand-in-hand, are the key to being sensitive to the Spirit's leading, which is the key to a victorious Christian life!

When you are sensitive to His leading you will be quick to confess your sin and receive forgiveness, allowing you to have unbroken fellowship with our Lord.

(Then you have power to forgive others!)

Remember—you don't have to pray out loud to be heard. He never leaves nor forsakes you and He hears your every thought and knows your every emotion.

Understanding this makes it possible to…

Rejoice always, pray without ceasing, in everything give thanks; for this is the will of God in Christ Jesus for you.
(1 Thessalonians 5:16-18)

As long as we are on THAT Scripture again ☺…

It's important that I mention:

These things I have spoken to you, that in Me you may have peace. In the world you will have tribulation; but be of good cheer, I have overcome the world."
(John 16:33)

Yep. You read that right. Tribulation is a promise from Jesus. But take heart and be joyful!

My brethren, count it all joy when you fall into various trials, knowing that the testing of your faith produces patience.
(James 1:2-3)

Why should we be joyful that our faith is being tested to grow patience? Glad you asked! ☺

But let patience have its perfect work, that you may be perfect and complete, lacking nothing.
(James 1:4)

And if you are struggling in the trial(s) you currently find yourself in? Fear not! He has provided the solution to that too!

If any of you lacks wisdom, let him ask of God, who gives to all liberally and without reproach, and it will be given to him.
(James 1:5)

There is only one condition:

But let him ask in faith, with no doubting, for he who doubts is like a wave of the sea driven and tossed by the wind.
(James 1:6)

Which brings us to this next important thing that I cannot leave out! (Isn't this exciting???)

But without faith it is impossible to please Him, for he who comes to God must believe that He is, and that He is a rewarder of those who diligently seek Him.
(Hebrews 11:6)

Faith. Faith is simply believing God. Believing what He says about Himself and His Son, and believing what He says about us.

In other words, trusting Him completely.

BUT...

Let's explore the word *believe* for a moment.

There are believers; and then there are BELIEVERS. ☺

The Bible says this about a certain group that believes that God is who he says He is:

You believe that there is one God. You do well. Even the demons believe – and tremble!
(James 2:19)

And the verse that follows that one says:

But do you want to know, O foolish man, that faith without works is dead?
(James 2:20)

Works are simply actions. If you look out your window in the morning, and see a very dark sky looming overhead, you would probably believe it was going to rain.

So you would take an umbrella for your walk to the bus stop, right?

That's an action based on your belief. You have a strong a belief and you adjusted your life accordingly.

When you say you believe God (have faith in Him), your actions should prove that.

If you say you believe God and He says that fornication (sex outside the bounds of marriage) is a sin, but you persist in it anyway, you really don't believe God.

Or you don't believe His word. Or what He says about the end result of sin.

You have no umbrella.

You may believe IN God, but you certainly don't believe God. Because He has spoken on that issue and you pay Him no regard.

The next verse I am going to share will make you jump for joy and do somersaults if you believe God!!! ☺

And the Scripture was fulfilled which says, "Abraham believed God, and it was accounted to him for righteousness." And he was called the friend of God.
(James 2:23)

Did you see that??? Friend of God.

OMG!!!
(Omigosh! ☺)

Counted as righteous and considered a friend of God because you believe Him! It blows my mind!

Of course, you should know that when you become God's friend, you inherit God's enemies.
Jesus said THIS:

You are My friends if you do whatever I command you. No longer do I call you servants, for a servant does not know what his master is doing; but I have called you friends, for all things that I heard from My Father I have made known to you.

These things I command you, that you love one another.
(John 15:14-15,17)

And He followed that up with THIS:

"If the world hates you, you know that it hated Me before it hated you. If you were of the world, the world would love its own.

Yet because you are not of the world, but I chose you out of the world, therefore the world hates you.

Remember the word that I said to you, 'A servant is not greater than his master.' If they persecuted Me, they will also persecute you.

If they kept My word, they will keep yours also. But all these things they will do to you for My name's sake, because they do not know Him who sent Me.
(John 15:18-21)

Now before you get your boxing gloves on to beat-up all God's enemies for Him,

We need to remember that not too long ago, we were His enemies, too. And how did He treat us?

Just like you learned in the early pages of your reading adventure…

But God demonstrates His own love toward us, in that while we were still sinners, Christ died for us.
(Romans 5:8)

We are to love our enemies. Whether they are our enemies because we are God's friend, or because of some other reason, we need to love them.

The loving heart of Jesus is forgiveness toward us. Remember?

See here what Jesus said:

"You have heard that it was said, 'You shall love your neighbor and hate your enemy.'

But I say to you, love your enemies, bless those who curse you, do good to those who hate you, and pray for those who spitefully use you and persecute you,

that you may be sons of your Father in heaven; for He makes His sun rise on the evil and on the good, and sends rain on the just and on the unjust.

For if you love those who love you, what reward have you? Do not even the tax collectors do the same?

And if you greet your brethren only, what do you do more than others? Do not even the tax collectors do so? Therefore you shall be perfect, just as your Father in heaven is perfect.
(Matthew 5:43-48)

Aaaah. Love. Let's talk about love, shall we?

He who does not love does not know God, for God is love.
(1 John 4:8)

At the heart of it all, God is love.

Because He loves, He wants to forgive.

Because He loves, He wants reconciliation.

Because He loves, He is merciful.

Because He loves, He is gracious.

Because He loves, He sent Jesus to die.

He cannot help but love, because He IS love!

The Bible is full of examples of God's love, and Jesus of course, is the highest expression of His love toward us.

But there is also a beautiful description given to us in Bible. Looky, looky! ☺

Love suffers long and is kind; love does not envy; love does not parade itself, is not puffed up;

does not behave rudely, does not seek its own, is not provoked, thinks no evil; does not rejoice in iniquity,

but rejoices in the truth; bears all things, believes all things, hopes all things, endures all things.

Love never fails.

(1 Corinthians 13:4-8a)

I told you it was beautiful!

Friend, thank you for bearing with me this far. I am almost done with this letter.

There is so much more I would love to share, but the purpose of this whole adventure was to introduce you to the Savior who loved you so much He died for you; and to equip you with what you need to begin your own journey with Him.

That being said, there are a couple more things I'd like to add before I sign off.

Worship. Everybody worships something or someone.

The website for the Merriam-Webster dictionary has several definitions for the word, but we'll stick with the ones for the verb (action) form.

1: to honor or show reverence for as a divine being or supernatural power

2: to regard with great or extravagant respect, honor, or devotion

Surely by now you think our Lord is worthy of such extravagant respect, honor, and devotion.

In our culture, people worship Hollywood celebrities, politicians, money, power, and of course, the all-time favorite — themselves.

We were created to worship our Creator. Worship takes many forms in different churches, and is expressed differently through different lives, yet in Christ, there is one common truth:

"But the hour is coming, and now is, when the true worshipers will worship the Father in spirit and truth; for the Father is seeking such to worship Him.

God is Spirit, and those who worship Him must worship in spirit and truth."
(John 4:23-24)

If you are in Christ, you have the Holy Spirit and as you follow His leading, your whole life will be worship to Him.

The God who calls you to worship Him —
and Him alone — equips you with what
you need to do what He desires of you.

Amazing, right?! Give thanks and
praise!!

As far as churches go, some have
elaborate and fancy rituals, and some are
just a group of believers meeting in home
or public park.

The question is not how does your church
worship, but does your life worship?

Finally, let's talk about the grace of God.

*For by grace you have been saved through
faith, and that not of yourselves; it is the gift
of God, not of works, lest anyone should
boast.*
*For we are His workmanship, created in
Christ Jesus for good works, which God
prepared beforehand that we should walk in
them.* **(Ephesians 2:8-10)**

The grace of God. The freely given, and
unmerited favor of God.

Here is an acronym commonly used to describe this grace...

God's

Riches

At

Christ's

Expense

This sums up everything God offers us.

As you read the Bible for yourself, you will discover many more riches included in your inheritance with Christ.

But never forget—it's ALL grace.

God, in His mercy, has redeemed you out of the slavery of sin at great cost to Himself.

There is nothing you can do to earn forgiveness.

Nothing you can do to earn your salvation.

It is a gift. It is grace.

The good works (actions/deeds) that *God prepared beforehand for you to walk in* are your response to His grace.

His Spirit will lead you into the works prepared specifically for you!

And while some people will get caught up in thinking the more publicity you get and the more your name is known, the greater your success…

That is not true in God's economy.

The call to work at McDonald's is just as important as the call to pastor a church.

God has reasons for having you where you are. And a main one is to share the Good News with the people He surrounds you with.

You don't need a special talent or gifting to tell someone what Jesus has done for you. Just a willing heart.
I read this somewhere a long time ago:

Christianity is one beggar telling another beggar where to find bread.

It wasn't in the Bible, but is surely sums up what sharing the Gospel of Jesus Christ looks like!

If you've found bread…

Go tell someone!!!

Let the redeemed of the Lord say so,
Whom He has redeemed from the hand of the
enemy,

And gathered out of the lands,
From the east and from the west,
From the north and from the south.
(Psalm 107:2-3)

That is the calling of our Jesus for us.

He doesn't long for just you and I to know the truth; He died for everyone who will come to Him.

But if we don't tell people, who will? Look at a prayer Jesus asks us to pray:

But when He saw the multitudes, He was
moved with compassion for them, because
they were weary and scattered, like sheep
having no shepherd.

Then He said to His disciples, "The harvest
truly is plentiful, but the laborers are few.
Therefore pray the Lord of the harvest to
send out laborers into His harvest."
(Matthew 9:36-38)

My prayer is that if you gave your life to Christ through our journey together, you would please enter into His harvest.

My other prayer for you if you gave your life to Christ through our journey together, is a Scripture prayer that you can find in Colossians 1:9-14:

For this reason I also, since the day I heard it, do not cease to pray for you, and to ask that you may be filled with the knowledge of His will in all wisdom and spiritual understanding;

that you may walk worthy of the Lord, fully pleasing Him, being fruitful in every good work and increasing in the knowledge of God;

strengthened with all might, according to His glorious power, for all patience and longsuffering with joy;

giving thanks to the Father who has qualified us to be partakers of the inheritance of the saints in the light.

And on that note, I shall thank you so much for allowing me this great honor,

and privilege. I hope to see you in
eternity!

I pray this has been as wonderful an
experience for you as it has been for me!
Grace and peace and blessings to you,

Beloved of the Lord ☺

Of Utmost Importance is...

The Return of Jesus

The Lord Jesus Christ is coming back someday! Many of us believe it will be soon! ☺

Because even the best Christian scholars God has given us do not agree on the details, I am not going to go into detail on what I believe about this most awesome event.

I am simply going to show you some Scriptures that tell us that He IS coming back! (And then give you a resource. ☺)

When the resurrected Jesus left earth, the angels said this to His followers:

"Men of Galilee, why do you stand gazing up into heaven? This same Jesus, who was taken up from you into heaven, will so come in like manner as you saw Him go into heaven."
(Acts 1:11)

There is also His own declaration about Himself:

"I am the Alpha and the Omega, the Beginning and the End," says the Lord, "who is and who was and who is to come, the Almighty."
(Revelation 1:8)

And I'll add two on how we are to conduct ourselves in light of this thrilling news:

And now, little children, abide in Him, that when He appears, we may have confidence and not be ashamed before Him at His coming.
(1 John 2:28)

And let us consider one another in order to stir up love and good works, not forsaking the assembling of ourselves together, as is the manner of some, but exhorting one another, and so much the more as you see the Day approaching.
(Hebrews 10:24-25)

If you want to explore the four different views on how and when this glorious return will take place, head down to your local Christian bookstore and ask to see their...

Rose Publishing Pamphlets

(Or type that into Amazon)

These little pamphlets are great, cover a wide variety of topics, and are excellent tools for both new and seasoned believers. And they are very reasonably priced!

They also have some books. Anything you buy from them is rock solid. ☺

At any rate, look for the one titled *Four Views of the End Times.*

(Be sure to look at all the other titles, too!)

Regarding Your Bible

Regarding Your Bible

There are quite a few different translations of the Bible.

There are more out there than I am going to list, and by all means take a look! Ask Him to help you select the one HE wants you to have! ☺

The King James Version (KJV)
Reads like Shakespeare's stuff.

The New King James Version (NKJV)
The King James Version in modern English.

Both are about an 11th or 12th grade reading level.

The New Living Translation (NLT)
Basic, easy-to-read English.

About a 6th grade reading level.

The International Children's Bible (ICB)
A translation created for children, but also good if English is your second language or you are not a strong reader.

It comes in different covers and not all of them give the appearance of belonging to a child.

(I don't think it's anything to be embarrassed about, but I know some people feel that way. I'm just happy to see people reading the Bible at all!)

Written for ages 7 and up.

There are lots of places online to read various translations. Two that I like a lot are:

www.biblegateway.com
(Very easy to navigate!)

www.blueletterbible.com
(They even have an app for your phone that let's you listen to the Bible! And it's free!)

Also, regarding your Bible...

Be a Berean!

Then the brethren immediately sent Paul and Silas away by night to Berea. When they arrived, they went into the synagogue of the Jews.

These were more fair-minded than those in Thessalonica, in that they received the word with all readiness, and searched the Scriptures daily to find out whether these things were so.
(Acts 17:10-12)

Never assume what you are being taught is true! Make sure it is in the Bible!

If you are in a land where Bibles are forbidden, yet somehow you got this book, praise God for the 300 or so verses you have in here!

And take heart, my persecuted Brothers and Sisters, for this promise remains:

It is written in the prophets, 'And they shall all be taught by God.' Therefore everyone who has heard and learned from the Father comes to Me. (John 6:45)

Regarding the Real Jesus

The following pages are not an attack on the people caught up in these organizations. They have been deceived by our enemy and we need to pray for them.

We are simply going to be Berean and bring some false teachings about Jesus to the light of His word for examination. ☺

Regarding the Jesus of the Jehovah's Witnesses

We will begin with a group known as the **Jehovah's Witnesses**. They are also known as the Watchtower Bible and Tract Society.

You have probably seen their Watchtower magazines/pamphlet thingies around or been handed one when they knocked on your door.

They also set up on sidewalks sometimes or in front of stores.

They teach a lot of things that are contrary to Scripture (resources to follow), but we are going to focus on the things regarding Jesus, because...

The greatest preacher in the Bible (besides Jesus, of course ☺) says this:

For I am jealous for you with godly jealousy. For I have betrothed you to one husband, that I may present you as a chaste virgin to Christ.

But I fear, lest somehow, as the serpent deceived Eve by his craftiness, so your minds may be corrupted from the simplicity that is in Christ.

For if he who comes preaches another Jesus whom we have not preached, or if you receive a different spirit which you have not received, or a different gospel which you have not accepted — you may well put up with it!
(2 Corinthians 11:2-4)

Don't put up with it; be Berean! ☺

Regarding Jesus, the Watchtower organization teaches:

1) Jesus is not God in the flesh, but a created being (Michael the Archangel).

But the Bible says this:

For in Him dwells all the fullness of the Godhead bodily;
(Colossians 2:9)

The New Living Translation (NLT) puts it like this:

For in Christ lives all the fullness of God in
a human body.
(Colossians 2:9)

2) That Jesus was not resurrected
   bodily, but as a spirit being.

But the Bible says this:

Behold My hands and My feet, that it is I
Myself. Handle Me and see, for a spirit does
not have flesh and bones as you see I have."
(Luke 24:39)

3) That Jesus returned invisibly to
   help set up their organization.

But the Bible says of His return:

Then the sign of the Son of Man will appear
in heaven, and then all the tribes of the earth
will mourn, and they will see the Son of
Man coming on the clouds of heaven with
power and great glory.
(Matthew 24:30)

4) That Jesus should not be given
   worship, but only honored as
   Jehovah's first creation.

But the Bible says this:

*Then He said to Thomas, "Reach your finger
here, and look at My hands; and reach your
hand here, and put it into My side. Do not
be unbelieving, but believing."*

*And Thomas answered and said to Him,
"My Lord and my God!"*
(John 20:27-28)

And Jesus did not rebuke Thomas!

(Alert! They have their own bible, called
the New World Translation. It is rejected
by all true Christian Hebrew and Greek
scholars.)

(It should also be noted that "Jehovah" is
a legitimate name of God. Get the Rose
Publishing pamphlet, *Names of God*! ☺)

Regarding the Jesus of Mormonism

Mormonism is trickier to address than the Watchtower Society.

First of all, they call themselves The Church of Jesus Christ of Latter-Day Saints.

And if you go to their official website, what they say at the outset sure sounds like everything we've been learning all along.

But let's get to the heart of the matter — who is the Jesus that they are talking about, and is He the same Jesus revealed in the Bible?

Before we look at that, you should know…

That Mormonism was founded by a guy who claimed that an angel appeared to him. That's where it all started.

(Remember what we learned about Satan "masquerading as an angel of light"?)

Here are some words from that greatest preacher (besides Jesus ☺) again:

But even if we, or an angel from heaven, preach any other gospel to you than what we have preached to you, let him be accursed.
(Galatians 1:8)

He feels so strongly about this that he repeats it!

As we have said before, so now I say again, if anyone preaches any other gospel to you than what you have received, let him be accursed.
(Galatians 1:9)

The "Heavenly Father" they refer to is "Elohim," which is a legitimate name of our God.

However, **their** Elohim was once a man who elevated himself to the position of a god, and now lives on a planet called Kolob.

He has many spiritual wives, and lots of spiritual sex, resulting in lots of spiritual children.

Those spiritual children are then born into human bodies.

This is <u>NOT</u> our Elohim.

Their teachings claim that the universe is populated with these men who became gods of their own planets, and their Elohim is merely one of them.

But <u>our</u> Elohim says this:

> *Remember the former things of old,*
> *For I am God, and there is no other;*
> *I am God, and there is none like Me,*
> **(Isaiah 46:9)**

They also teach that every man has the potential to become one of these gods.

Which is the lie the serpent told Eve (remember) taken up a notch. Eve was told the fruit would make them "like" God. Mormonism says you can actually "be" a god.

Back to their Jesus…

They claim that Jesus was one of Elohim's spirit children, and that Elohim actually visited earth to have sex with Mary, so that Jesus would have a physical body.

But the Bible says this:

Then the angel said to her, "Do not be afraid, Mary, for you have found favor with God. And behold, you will conceive in your womb and bring forth a Son, and shall call His name Jesus.
(Luke 1:30-31)

Then Mary said to the angel, "How can this be, since I do not know a man?"

And the angel answered and said to her, "The Holy Spirit will come upon you, and the power of the Highest will overshadow you; therefore, also, that Holy One who is to be born will be called the Son of God.
(Luke 1:34-35)

And then, because Jesus was simply one of their Elohim's spiritual children (like they claim we all are), so was Lucifer, also known as Satan (remember what we learned about him?).

But our Jesus is the only unique Son of God. He is part of what is called "The Trinity."

You will not find that word in the Bible, but it is used to describe the relationship between God the Father, God the Son, and God the Holy Spirit.

God exists in a Trinity of three eternal and co-equal persons.

God the Father:

Grace to you and peace from God our Father and the Lord Jesus Christ.
(1 Corinthians 1:3)

God the Son (you've seen this before ☺):

For in Him dwells all the fullness of the Godhead bodily;
(Colossians 2:9)

And finally (drum roll please ☺)…

God the Holy Spirit:
But Peter said, "Ananias, why has Satan filled your heart to lie to the Holy Spirit and

keep back part of the price of the land for
yourself?

While it remained, was it not your own?
And after it was sold, was it not in your
own control? Why have you conceived this
thing in your heart?

You have not lied to men but to God."
(Acts 5:3-4)

And to sum it all up, right before our
resurrected Lord went up to heaven, He
had some parting words for His
followers:

Go therefore and make disciples of all the
nations, baptizing them in the name of the
Father and of the Son and of the Holy Spirit,
(Matthew 28:19)

All of this should have surely shown you
the difference between the Jesus of the
Bible and the Jesus of the Book of
Mormon.

(Alert! They also have two other books
they draw from: The Pearl of Great Price,
and Doctrine and Covenants.)

And all of this should have really encouraged you to want to…

Be a Berean! ☺

It's like being a bank teller.

They study the real money until they know it so well that a counterfeit bill is obvious at first glance.

That being said, if you are wanting a short, easy read on false teachings, grab a copy of *Fast Facts on False Teachings*, by Ron Carlson & Ed Decker.

If you are the scholarly type, *The Kingdom of the Cults*, by Walter Martin.

Regarding the Jesus of the Prosperity Gospel

This is a most devious deception that has trapped many true Christians. Please pay close attention.

"Beware of false prophets, who come to you in sheep's clothing, but inwardly they are ravenous wolves."
(Matthew 7:15)

But there were also false prophets among the people, even as there will be false teachers among you, who will secretly bring in destructive heresies, even denying the Lord who bought them, and bring on themselves swift destruction.
(2 Peter 2:1)

For when they speak great swelling words of emptiness, they allure through the lusts of the flesh, through lewdness, the ones who have actually escaped from those who live in error.
(2 Peter 2:18)

For the time will come when they will not endure sound doctrine, but according to

their own desires, because they have itching ears, they will heap up for themselves teachers; and they will turn their ears away from the truth, and be turned aside to fables.
(2 Timothy 4:3-4)

I am going to put that last one here again, but this time from The New Living Translation (NLT).

For a time is coming when people will no longer listen to sound and wholesome teaching.

They will follow their own desires and will look for teachers who will tell them whatever their itching ears want to hear. They will reject the truth and chase after myths.
(2 Timothy 4:3-4 NLT)

There are a lot of "preachers" out there today that are very visible, and very "successful" in the eyes of the world.

They have multi-million dollar homes, private jets, luxurious cars and drivers, and more money than they will ever spend.

They say it is God's blessing upon them for believing His promises, and that He wants you to be blessed like they are.

Do not listen to them. They worship at the altars of Self and the Almighty Dollar. They have never read these words of Jesus:

Then He said to them all, "If anyone desires to come after Me, let him deny himself, and take up his cross daily, and follow Me.
(Luke 9:23)

They have Jesus confused with Santa Claus, and the Gospel of Jesus Christ confused with the American Dream.

If God blesses you financially, by all means rejoice and celebrate; but celebrate that He has counted you worthy to further His Kingdom, which revolves around populating it with repentant sinners! ☺

Taking the gospel to your neighborhood and the world.

He has counted you worthy to feed hungry people in His name, and to clothe

129

poor people in His name; in short, if He blesses you financially, it's so that you can be a blessing to others.

In His name.

Not so you can build your own little kingdom here on earth.

Nothing you accumulate here on earth is going with you when you die. The only thing you are leaving earth with is your soul.

And that's why Jesus died. To save your soul. And He has called you (wherever you are positioned in life) to join Him in His work.

If God chooses to bless you financially, you best be listening closely for what He wants you to do with the money!

Here is a warning that many "teachers" out there today should heed:

Come now, you rich, weep and howl for your miseries that are coming upon you! Your riches are corrupted, and your garments are moth-eaten.

Your gold and silver are corroded, and their corrosion will be a witness against you and will eat your flesh like fire. You have heaped up treasure in the last days.
(James 5:1-3)

You have lived on the earth in pleasure and luxury; you have fattened your hearts as in a day of slaughter.
(James 5:5)

Their Jesus is not the same Jesus you have learned about from me.

Our Jesus says this:

"Do not lay up for yourselves treasures on earth, where moth and rust destroy and where thieves break in and steal;

but lay up for yourselves treasures in heaven, where neither moth nor rust destroys and where thieves do not break in and steal.

For where your treasure is, there your heart will be also."
(Matthew 6:19-21)

They sound like they know what they are talking about because they quote Scripture verses, BUT they are usually taken out of context.

Also, they talk a lot about claiming the promises of God, but they mainly mean the ones that they can throw together to make it sound like God approves **their message**:

God wants you to have health, wealth, and prosperity. He wants you to have what YOU think is best.

In reality...

God wants you to have faith, trust, love, holiness, humility, hope, peace, gentleness, kindness, self-control, generosity, and a host of other things that He promises to provide through His Spirit.

He is much more interested in your eternal security than your temporary comfort.

He is much more interested in conforming you to the image of His Son and building His character into you than He is in turning you into a celebrity.

Does this nullify His promise to provide for your needs?

In no way.

What God thinks you need to be conformed to His image may not be what you think you need.

In fact, I can promise you that they probably aren't the same at all. LOL ☺

And whatever God is doing in your life, He is preparing you for the next step.

Gotta trust Him! ☺

And as you read the Bible, you'll find that a lot of the people He used the most to get His word out, went through the worst trials ever!

They knew God as the Great Comforter because they needed His comfort. They knew Him as the Great Provider because they needed provision.

Whatever God wants to prove Himself to be in your life, you have to be in a place to learn it!

That's why we can count it all joy when we face trials and tribulations! (Remember? ☺)

You will never see the amazing hand of God come through for you, if you are not in a situation where you need Him to do so.

And every time that happens, your faith increases; and your mind explodes with wonder and your heart bows down in awe!

That is the Jesus I've shared with you! ☺

One last thing on prosperity — it is not money that is the root of all evil. The Bible says it is "the love of money" that is.

For the love of money is a root of all kinds of evil, for which some have strayed from the faith in their greediness, and pierced themselves through with many sorrows.
(1 Timothy 6:10)

Being wealthy is not a sin; being greedy is.

One More Thing

Lastly, I encourage you to seek a church where the pastor has his Bible open and is encouraging you to have yours open as well.

If someone gave you this book, I am hoping that they added church contact info to it somewhere. ☺

But in case they forgot, pray about it. If you don't feel the Lord leading you one way or another, see if you can find a Calvary Chapel.

There are lots of churches streaming on YouTube, and with lots of their sermons posted on their websites.

Pastor Jeff of Calvary Chapel Yakima just finished up the Gospel of John (on YouTube). That's a great place to start.

And speaking of the Bible, I want you to know that it is a big book separated into 66 little books.

Under your table of contents you will see "The Old Testament" and "The New Testament."

The Old Testament stuff all takes place before Jesus came to earth.

Then there are 400 years of silence from God.

Then the New Testament is about Jesus and what happened after His resurrection. (Mostly letters by an important guy named Paul. ☺)

The first four books of the New Testament are called the Gospels and are testimonies about Jesus' life and ministry on earth.

If the Lord does not lead you to start somewhere else, I suggest you start with the Gospels. (Matthew, Mark, Luke, and John.)

If you are wondering why you should consider the Bible a reliable source of information, please pick up a copy of *Evidence that Demands a Verdict*, by Josh McDowell and Sean McDowell.

It addresses that and much more! I personally think every believer should have one! ☺

A Fond Farewell

Dear Friend,

Well, it is time to bid you a most fond farewell.

The moment is bittersweet; I have much more I would love to share, but it is time for your discovery of the Joy-of-Jesus to begin.!

I thank you from the bottom of my heart for allowing me this privilege.

I also thank you for overlooking any punctuation/grammar errors. I somehow managed to graduate high school, but really showed up very rarely once I had a driver's license (10th grade).

I also self-publish, and my books sometimes get a little off-base from what I want when I create the pdf file.

If I can't fix it in 3 tries, I throw up my hands and cry, "Grace! Grace unto it!" So if that happened in publishing this, please give me grace! ☺

I'm going to tell you a little about myself, not to glory in ME, but to glorify HIM, and hopefully encourage you.

After giving my life to Christ the first time in 1994, all of this happened:

A bad marriage filled with sexual deviancy, an ugly divorce, Acute Lymphoblastic Leukemia, two years of chemotherapy, 2 ½ weeks of brain radiation, 7 chemo treatments to the brain through my spine, mental illness,

quite a few extended all-expenses paid vacations to the psychiatric ward ☺, addiction, 2 arrests, 2 suicide attempts, about 5 serious psychotic episodes, broken friendships, several years of hypocrisy, and more.

And for the icing on the cake, while I was in the psyche ward after my first episode, my pastor was behind the pulpit preaching I had a demon!

(Being the demon-lady of a small town was quite a treat. LOL ☺ Of course I moved away, but mental illness moved with me!)

But the blessings! O the blessings!

Jesus never once left me, nor forsook me in all those years. Even the years I was the worst hypocrite ever.

Many of my problems (especially the hypocrisy) stemmed from lack of understanding of what sin was and how bad it is, and what it means to really follow Christ.

Hence, this book, born out of prayer that my experiences will help others.

Through it all…

He has divinely provided many, many times for my (and my daughter's) needs, including housing, food, employment, and clothing, and money, and of course, spiritual needs.

(Living on the fixed income of Social Security Disability gives the Lord LOTS of opportunity to pull through. LOL! ☺)

In fact, His provision has been so abundant and so obviously from His hand, that when my adult daughter (who currently does not follow Jesus) told her ex-boyfriend about me, she said:

"She has good luck with God." Now, you and I know it's not luck at all! ☺ But nonetheless, she saw His hand in my life.

Through all the trials and tribulations, I have learned to trust Him more and more.

The things I shared with you are things that I have learned from Jesus carrying me through all those things that seemed a curse.

I am grateful for every moment of it. I look back and see Him teaching me through the lives of others and my own experience—to trust Him completely, to have compassion, give forgiveness, show grace, speak the truth in love, and just everything He promises to teach us!

In short, my testimony is this:

The Lord Jesus has proven faithful to me, according to His mercy, according to His love, according to His grace, and according to His word.

He IS who He says He is.

He has proved it over and over in my life, and He is more amazing to me today than He was yesterday.

And I expect to say the same thing tomorrow. And the day after that.

As for me, I am simply an unremarkable, middle-aged, severely overweight (thank you psyche meds ☺) mother and grandmother with tan teeth (chain-smoker) and a goatee every other morning. LOL

Who happens to love the Lord her God with all her heart, soul, mind and strength, and desires to see His will done on earth—people entering His kingdom!

What is more than remarkable to me is that Jesus loves me with wholehearted abandon in ways I cannot even begin to understand.

The sovereign King of the Universe knows my name and cares about my struggles.

The Bible says he knows the number of hairs on my head.

I don't think we really have a word in any language on earth to adequately describe Him.

At least, I've never heard one. The best we've got is AWESOME!!!

So that's how I will say it. The real Jesus is AWESOME and walking through life with Him is AMAZING!

I pray you have entered into your own walk with the living Christ through what has been shared with you in this book.

I sign off with a final prayer for you, taken straight from the beloved Bible…

"The Lord bless you and keep you;
The Lord make His face shine upon you,
And be gracious to you;
The Lord lift up His countenance upon you,
And give you peace." '
(Numbers 6:24-26)

In the love of Christ,

-

Beloved of the Lord ☺

p.s.

Please carry your umbrella!